Ruff Translation

Paw-ket Dictionary
Dog to Human

JILLIAN BLUME

CENTENNIAL BOOKS

Ruff Translation

Paw-ket Dictionary
Dog to Human

Contents

What's in a Woof?

Our dogs communicate with us in many ways, from their barks to their wagging tails. Now, research is offering new insight into what exactly they are trying to say.

Dogs have been man's (and woman's) best friend for tens of thousands of years, but we still have a lot to learn about them. Over the past few decades, scientists, veterinarians and other animal experts have investigated a wide array of canine behaviors and cognition to better understand them.

Dogs are America's most popular pet, living in 38.4% of U.S. households (an estimated 76.8 million canine companions), according to the American Veterinary Medical Association. Our relationship with our dogs makes us healthier and happier, from lowering blood pressure and increasing physical activity to flooding both human and canine brains with oxytocin, the "love hormone."

The more humans understand what dogs' body language and vocalizations mean, the better we are able to make our best friends happy and keep them safe. Dogs have evolved to communicate with people, developing specific facial expressions and even a muscle that lifts their eyebrows so they can make those irresistible, heart-melting puppy eyes. But sadly, they can't speak in words to explain their body language, barks, whines and other noises, so it's up to us to learn their moves and vocabulary.

This book explores the nature of our relationship with our dogs and includes information on training, bonding, mood disorders, emotions, exercise needs, intelligence, developmental stages and more. You can read about nature vs. nurture, dogs' superpower sense of smell, licking and kissing, body language and barking, spaying and neutering, panting, personality, puppy development and historical facts such as the origin of guide dogs. You'll explore the remarkable world of our four-legged best friends so you can understand their language better and become the best human companion your dog believes you can be. —*Jillian Blume*

Adoption
(ə-ˈdäp-shən)

The act or process of acquiring a pet, especially a stray or abandoned animal, from an animal rescue organization. Adopting a dog from a shelter or rescue group not only saves the life of the dog you adopt, it also makes room so another animal's life can be saved. Shelters are filled with friendly dogs of all types, from purebreds to supermutts. The good news: The number of pet adoptions is on the rise, while euthanasia numbers are falling nationwide.

Who Knew?

According to the ASPCA, approximately 3.3 million dogs enter U.S. animal shelters nationwide every year; of those, about 1.6 million are adopted.

A

Adulthood
(ə-'dəlt-hủd)

The stage of development when dogs reach physical and emotional maturity. According to the American Kennel Club, puppies are officially considered adults when they reach 1 year of age, but experts say it's more complicated than that. The emotional and hormonal maturity and temperament of an adult dog often coincides with socialization, training and learning appropriate behavior with other dogs. Dogs may reach sexual maturity, meaning the ability to reproduce, before they become adults.

Who Knew?

Puppies reach their full size at between 1 and 2 years of age, depending on the breed.

Agility Training

(ə-ˈji-lə-tē ˈtrā-niŋ)

Training for a sport in which humans direct dogs through a timed obstacle course. Agility courses are designed to demonstrate a dog's athletic ability, conditioning and willingness to work with its handler. The exercises require physical prowess and mental concentration and include activities such as pole-weaving, tunnel-running and hurdle-jumping. Dogs that enjoy these drills are (not surprisingly) typically energetic, respond well to training and relish running and jumping.

Who Knew?

Breeds such as border collies, Shetland sheepdogs, Australian shepherds, golden retrievers, Jack Russell terriers and papillons often excel at agility competitions.

Anxiety

(aŋ-ˈzī-ə-tē)

Apprehension, nervousness or fear about an impending or perceived danger. Dogs may exhibit different types of anxiety, due to separation, noise sensitivity, environmental changes and resource guarding. Anxiety can sometimes be a reaction to a negative experience, a lack of early socialization or a traumatic environment, but there can also be a genetic tendency for some dogs to be naturally nervous. Signs include panting, pacing, whining, licking the lips or trembling. It may be helpful to consult a veterinarian or a behaviorist to learn strategies that can help your dog become less anxious.

Who Knew?

Regular exercise, some gentle massage and playing soothing music are all strategies that can help a dog feel calmer and more relaxed.

Baby Talk

(ˈbā-bē ˈtȯk)

The consciously altered speech—using a high pitch—that humans sometimes use in speaking to dogs. Baby talk is a natural instinct to connect with our dogs on a deeper level. Since dogs' understanding of words is limited, they may take cues from a human's pitch and tone. Dogs pay more attention to a high-pitched tone than a normal speaking one, especially when it includes words that they do understand (like "Good boy!").

Who Knew?

According to a study from the University of York in the United Kingdom, puppies showed a higher behavioral response to baby talk than adult dogs.

Bark

('bärk)

The characteristic short, loud cry of a dog. A dog's bark will differ depending on the situation, such as a disturbance (a doorbell ringing), being in isolation (locked outside away from its owner) and play, according to research from the late dog behaviorist Sophia Yin. She discovered that disturbance barks tend to be harsh, low frequency and varied, while isolation and play barks are more often tonal, higher frequency and modulated.

Who Knew?

According to dog behaviorist Stanley Coren, the most common form of barking is a rapid string of two to four barks, with pauses in between. "It's the classic alarm bark, meaning, 'Call the pack. There is something going on that should be looked into!'" he has explained.

Belly Rub

('be-lē 'rəb)

The act of massaging or scratching a dog's abdomen. A dog often indicates it wants a belly rub by rolling over onto its back and exposing its underside—a submissive behavior that shows how comfortable your pup feels. Some dogs enjoy belly rubs simply because they feel good, but they are also an opportunity for humans and dogs to bond.

Who Knew?

When a dog rolls onto its back in front of other canines, it usually indicates it wants to play. Researcher Alexandra Horowitz calls it a "self takedown" when a larger dog flops on the ground and reveals its belly for a smaller playmate to feel safe in approaching.

Body Language

('bä-dē 'laŋ-gwij)

The nonverbal communication that dogs use to express their emotions and intentions to humans and to other dogs, primarily through the mouth, eyes, tail and torso. They even have a muscle that lifts their eyebrows, just to make those heart-tugging expressions at us. Body language will also vary depending on the specific situation; an anxious dog at home may exhibit different body language than an anxious dog in a kennel. Dogs can also read body language, facial expressions and vocal tones in other canines.

Who Knew?

There are seven major areas with which your dog tries to communicate: eyes, ears, tail, mouth, hair, sweat/panting and body posture. Each should be viewed in relation to the others.

Bond

('bänd)

A uniting or binding force. Dogs and humans have a deep bond that dates back thousands of years. (There's evidence of a dog and human being buried together about 14,000 years ago.) While dogs and wolves share 99.9% of their mitochondrial DNA, there are a few high-sociability genes that dogs have that are similar to the sociability genes found in humans. Dogs also activate the release of the hormone oxytocin in humans—the same hormonal response that bonds us to our children.

Who Knew?

A study using MRI machines revealed the part of dogs' brains that light up when they hear their owners' voices is the same area of the human brain that engages when we are fond of someone or something.

Chew

('chü)

To crush, grind or gnaw something with the teeth. A dog's need to chew is hardwired; their powerful teeth were developed to take down prey in the wild. But there are other factors in their desire to gnaw. Chomping on bones helps to keep a dog's teeth clean. It also provides an outlet for excess energy. For puppies, it eases the pain of teething. And it's a way for dogs to explore their environment. Providing dogs with appropriate—and safe—toys helps to deter destructive behavior (and keep your best shoes intact!).

Who Knew?

A dog's bite strength depends on its size: Large dogs with big heads and wide jaws have the highest potential bite force. A mastiff, for example, has been measured as having a bite strength of 552 pounds—just shy of the bite force that a lion has, according to behaviorist Stanley Coren.

Crate Training

('krāt 'trā-niŋ)

The process used to train a dog to view its crate as a familiar, safe place, where it can retreat and relax. Crates are also often used in house-training because dogs dislike soiling their dens; the dog will learn to control its bladder while in the crate. Teaching dogs to enjoy their crates is also crucial in emergencies, in case you need to transport your animal into a safer environment, or in case of travel. But while crates can become a dog's safe haven, no dog should spend most of its time locked in one, and you should never use it as a form of punishment.

Who Knew?

Puppies younger than 6 months old should not stay in a crate for more than three to four hours because they can't control their bladders that long.

Cuddle

('kə-dəl)

To hold close for comfort or in affection. While not all dogs like to cuddle, those that do benefit from the extra warmth and love. Cuddling also gives dogs a way to protect and bond with their humans and acts as a stress reliever for dogs and their owners. Some breeds are more prone to enjoy cuddling than others, but each dog is an individual. However, most dogs do *not* enjoy being hugged around their necks.

Who Knew?

Stroking a dog for five to 24 minutes has been shown to increase levels of the "love" or "cuddle" hormone oxytocin in the bloodstream; the effect is greater if someone pets a familiar dog rather than a friendly yet unfamiliar dog.

Domesticated
(də-ˈme-sti-ˌkā-təd)

The process of adapting over time to life in close association with humans. While there are several theories, dogs are thought to have evolved from wolves that had a friendlier, less aggressive demeanor toward people (and learned to hang around and snack on their leftovers). But dogs still maintain some behaviors from their days of roaming wild, including the instinct to den and to chew. The physical changes that appeared in dogs over time, such as curly tails and floppy ears, is a process known as self-domestication, when the friendliest animals in a species gain an advantage.

Who Knew?

Scientists place the domestication of dogs sometime between 20,000 and 40,000 years ago.

Dominance

('dä-mə-nən(t)s)

The state of commanding or controlling others. Dominance in dogs can be seen through both behavior and body language, such as herding people and other pets by biting at their ankles, standing over another dog, guarding food and toys, and growling at strangers. But aggressive behavior often stems from fear and anxiety rather than dominance. Animal behaviorists recommend training with positive reinforcement to communicate rules and boundaries to a dominant dog, rather than trying to exert your own dominance over the animal.

Who Knew?

Wolves vying for the alpha position in the pack hierarchy is an instinctual action that still manifests in some dogs.

Dream

('drēm)

Thoughts, images and emotions that occur during sleep. Dogs do appear to dream, but scientists can only speculate what they are thinking about. Researcher Stanley Coren posits that breed-specific activities may take place in their dreams: A Labrador retriever is more likely to dream about chasing tennis balls than a pug. Judging by dogs that appear to be running in place as they sleep, pups may also dream about events that occurred that day or at another time in their lives. Dogs also seem to have nightmares, though we'll never know for sure.

Who Knew?

Waking a dog from a deep sleep can be dangerous, as they may be disoriented and react aggressively. It's best to let them be. (Thus the expression, "Let sleeping dogs lie.")

Emotions
(i-'mō-shənz)

A mental reaction experienced as a strong feeling. Once thought to be incapable of having feelings, we now know that canines (and other animals) can have a variety of emotions. Dogs possess the same brain structures that produce emotions and produce the same chemical changes seen in the human brain when exhibiting certain emotions. Researchers believe that the mind of a dog is equal to that of a 2½-year-old child, including the basic emotions of joy, anger, fear, disgust and love.

Who Knew?

According to the American Kennel Club, dogs can sense our emotions and read our facial expressions. They instinctively know when their humans are happy, sad, nervous or stressed.

Eyesight

('ī-,sīt)

The process of seeing. A dog's eyes contain
only two types of cones (the receptors that
help with day vision and color perception),
which means they can only distinguish
blue-violet, yellow and shades of gray. They
also have less binocular vision than humans,
which provides depth perception, although
many breeds have an advantage of better
peripheral vision. Dogs are also nearsighted
with about 20/75 vision—they must be
20 feet from something to see it as well as
a human (with 20/20 vision) can at 75 feet.

Who Knew?

Dogs have the advantage over us with superior night
vision: Their eyes contain more rods, which act as
light receptors, as well as a membrane called the
tapetum lucidum, which reflects light back on the
retina (and produces that eerie glow you'll see in a
dog's eyes at night).

Fetch

('fech)

A game in which humans throw something for a dog to chase after and bring back. Many dogs love the high-energy endeavor— it's an opportunity to run fast and catch something, satisfying a dog's hunting instincts. Showing off their skills during a game of fetch also makes dogs feel good. And since you're both in on the action (that ball isn't going to throw itself!), the interactive nature strengthens the bond between human and dog.

Who Knew?

Breeds that tend to love to play fetch the most include border collies, Labrador retrievers, golden retrievers, Australian shepherds, standard poodles and Weimaraners.

Food Motivated

(ˈfüd ˈmō-tə-ˌvā-təd)

Dogs that are driven to do something by the promise of food. Food-motivated dogs are easily trained by using small amounts of high-value treats, such as a piece of cooked chicken or freeze-dried liver. Try this if you are trying to teach a food-motivated dog how to sit: Hold the treat directly in front of its nose, then move the treat up and back over its head. The dog's nose will follow the treat, which naturally causes its body to move into a sit position (at which point you can give it the reward). If your dog isn't entirely food motivated, it may also respond to using toys as a way to train with positive reinforcement.

Who Knew?

Labrador retrievers are known for being very (very!) food motivated.

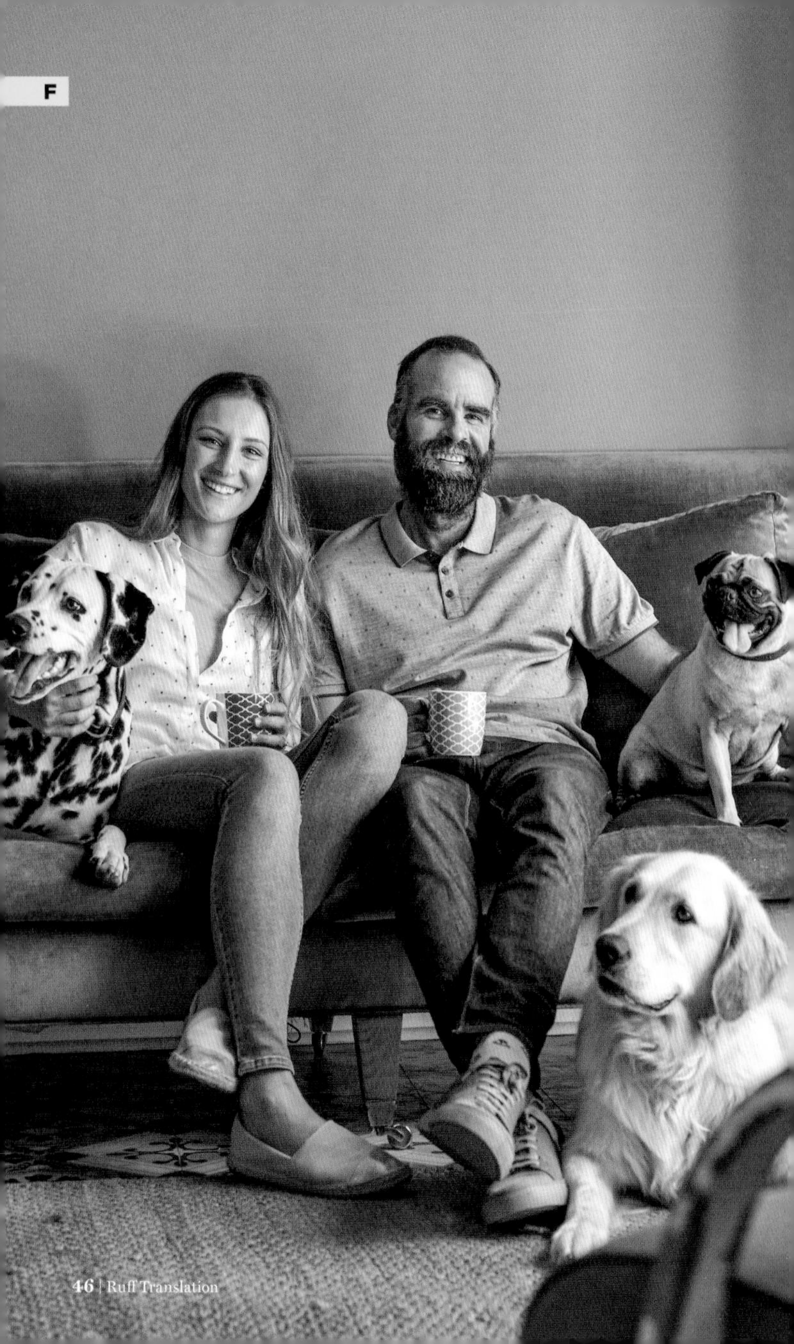

Foster

('fȯ-st(ə-)r)

To give shelter and care to a dog until they are adopted. Fostering dogs gets them out of the shelter environment and into a home. It helps dogs recover both mentally and physically, while getting them used to being part of a family. For dogs that are extremely stressed in a shelter environment, fostering may even save them from euthanasia. A dog that is cat- or dog-friendly can be fostered in a home with another pet. Fostering a dog gives the shelter or rescue more information, so they can find it a perfect forever home.

Who Knew?

Dogs that are adopted by their foster parent are known as "foster fails"—which is actually a great outcome!

Groom

('grŭm)

To bathe and maintain one's appearance. All dogs need regular grooming to keep their coat, eyes, ears and teeth healthy. Dogs can largely be groomed at home, although some signature haircuts (looking at you, standard poodle) are best done by a professional. Grooming is essential for the health and comfort of dogs, especially for longhaired breeds whose fur or hair can become matted. Basic grooming should include frequently brushing the coat, trimming the nails and cleaning out the eyes and ears. Regular dental care is also important.

Who Knew?

When a dog's coat becomes matted, it's more than just a beauty issue: Matting pulls at a dog's sensitive skin and can become extremely painful, making it difficult for a dog to move around.

Guide Dogs

('gīd 'dȯgz)

Assistance dogs trained to lead visually impaired people around obstacles. The first guide dog in the U.S. was trained in 1928 by Morris Frank, a 19-year-old blind man from Nashville, Tennessee, who had heard about an American woman in Switzerland, Dorothy Harrison Eustis, helping World War I veterans who'd lost their sight work with German shepherds. Frank traveled to Switzerland to work with Eustis and brought a female dog (whom he renamed Buddy) back home. Eustis and Frank later established The Seeing Eye school in 1929, helping to train other guide dogs.

Who Knew?

German shepherds, Labrador retrievers and golden retrievers are the most common breeds used as guide dogs.

Hackles

('ha-kəls)

The hairs that run along a dog's spine, starting from the back of the neck and down to the tail. While raising these hairs (known as hackling) is typically a dog's attempt to look bigger, it depends on the context. If the hackles are up and the dog is also growling and/or standing very still, it might be about to snap. But if the dog is running and jumping, it may simply be a sign of excitement.

Who Knew?

All dogs have hairs that feature this piloerection function (a tendency to rise up); it's just more obvious in some breeds than others.

Hearing

('hir-iŋ)

The process of perceiving sound. Dogs
are born deaf, but begin to hear at around
3 weeks old. Their sense of hearing is about
four times greater than humans. Dogs can
hear high-pitched sounds in the range of
47,000 to 65,000Hz (humans can only
hear up to 20,000Hz). Dogs can also hear
much softer sounds, which is why some
dogs can detect earthquakes by hearing
the high-pitched sound of underground
seismic activity.

Who Knew?

Dogs have much deeper ear canals than humans,
which create a better tunnel for sound to travel
down to the eardrums. They have 18 muscles
controlling the ears that move to capture sound,
and each ear moves independently of the other.

Heartworm

('härt-wərm)

A parasite transmitted by mosquitoes that invades the heart and pulmonary arteries of dogs. Dogs are a natural host for heartworms, which live in their bodies and reproduce, growing up to a foot long. A dog's body can hold hundreds of heartworms. Left untreated, the parasite can cause lasting damage to the lungs, heart and other organs, and it can eventually lead to death. Heartworms can affect a dog's health and quality of life even after treatment.

Who Knew?

The best treatment for heartworms is prevention, including monthly chewable tablets, topical medication, or an injectable medication that is given every six or 12 months.

Housebreak

('haús 'brāk)

The process of teaching a dog to eliminate in the right place. There are several effective ways to housebreak a dog, but they all require consistency and positive reinforcement. Crate training helps a puppy's muscles develop to hold its bladder and bowels. Some people train their dogs to use puppy pads as well as to go outdoors. The best way to housebreak your dog is to schedule numerous walks throughout the day and evening (ideally at least every two hours); the frequency will depend on the dog's age, breed and previous training.

Who Knew?

Never punish a dog for accidents by hitting, yelling or rubbing their nose in it. This will only make the dog afraid of you, and it significantly increases their stress around a basic bodily function.

Instinct

('in-ˌstiŋ(k)t)

A natural or inherent aptitude or impulse. Behavior that is instinctual in dogs includes marking their territory, licking their puppies or other dogs they feel protective toward, herding behavior (in herding breeds), digging holes, carrying things in their mouth (particularly retrievers), hunting and even playing (where puppies learn to stalk, pounce and grab). Some dogs instinctively spin around before lying down as they did when they lived in the wild, patting down the grass and kicking away any debris and bugs.

Who Knew?

Some dogs have a smelly instinct—they love to roll in dead animals or other strongly scented things. It's an instinct that developed as a way to camouflage their odor in order to sneak up on their prey.

Intelligence

(in-'te-lə-jən(t)s)

The ability to learn or understand. Canine intelligence has three major dimensions: instinctive intelligence, adaptive intelligence, and working and obedience intelligence, according to behaviorist Stanley Coren. Dogs' intelligence can be measured by their ability to learn and do work, whether it's hunting, guarding livestock, doing tricks or simply obeying commands. The faster dogs learn, the smarter they are likely to be.

Who Knew?

A study published in the journal *Cell* revealed that dogs can read human facial expressions and make decisions based on them, proving that they have a high level of emotional intelligence.

menswaeardog ⊙ ...

♡ ۹ ⊽ 🔖
9,424 likes
menswaeardog Feral Bueller's Day Off 😎

manny_the_frenchie ⊙ ...

6,786 likes
manny_the_frenchie Hey girl, just got a new Valentine's day harness, wanna cuddle?! 🍫 ... more
View all 51 comments

tunameltsmyheart ⊙ ...

♡ ۹ ⊽ 🔖
22,975 likes
tunameltsmyheart If someone you love LOVES Tuna in oversized glasses and a Hawaiian shirt, or loves Trader Joe's in general, Tuna's... more

norbertthedog ⊙ ...

♡ ۹ ⊽ 🔖
21,232 likes
norbertthedog splish splash 🛁

Internet-Famous Dogs

(ˈin-tər-ˌnet ˈfā-məs dägz)

Dogs that have attained wide recognition through social media. You may recognize some of these famous faces thanks to Instagram, Facebook, YouTube and other platforms. Consider Menswear Dog, a Shiba Inu called "The Most Stylish Dog in the World"; Manny the Frenchie, "author" of *Manny the Frenchie's Art of Happiness* and the world's most-followed bulldog; Norbert, a 3-pound therapy dog with his tongue permanently sticking out; and Tuna, the chiweenie, with his visible overbite.

Who Knew?

One of the first canine internet celebrities was Boo, an adorable Pomeranian that had more than 16 million Facebook likes. Her owner set up her Facebook page in 2009; Boo died in January 2019.

Jump

(ˈjəmp)

To spring into the air. Usually, the motivation for dogs to jump is to greet a human face-to-face. Some dogs may leap to express their exuberance; others may just find it fun (just Google "dogs on trampolines"). The behavior is often a way to get a person's attention and say, "Hey! Look at me!" although it can easily become a behavioral problem and may cause injury, especially with young children. Jumping is also part of a dog's instinctual predatory behavior, which includes hunting, stalking and pouncing on prey.

Who Knew?

Large, muscular dogs such as greyhounds, wolfhounds and vizslas can easily jump as high as 6 feet from a standing start.

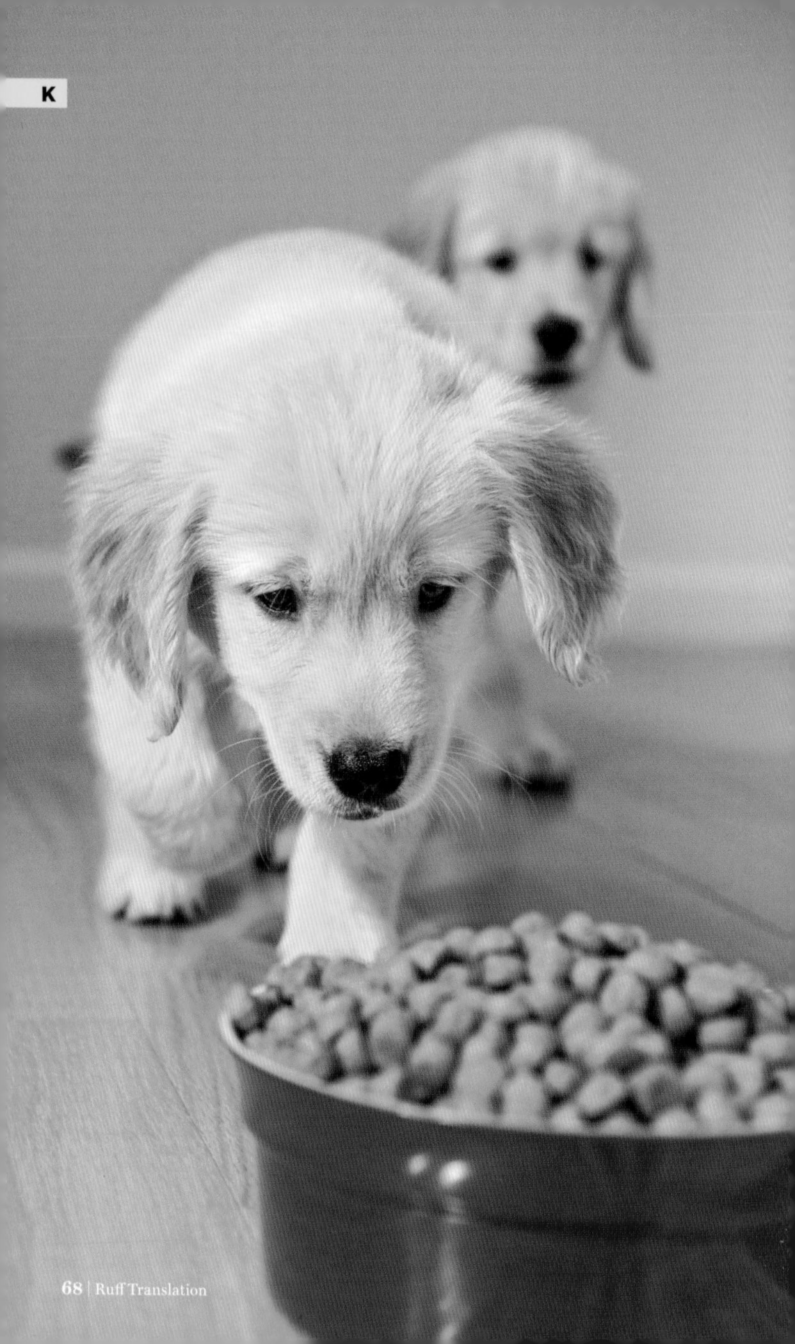

Kibble
('ki-bəl)

Small, dried pellets of processed food.
Kibble is often less expensive than canned or
cooked-fresh food and easier to store. Most
dry dog food is supplemented with vitamins,
minerals and other nutrients depending on
a dog's age, size and health requirements. In
general, dried food is better for dental health
but may have more artificial ingredients
and is generally not as flavorful as canned
or fresh food. The best diet may be a mix of
both wet and dry, but talk to your vet about
what your pooch might need.

Who Knew?

Kibble was invented in 1860 by James Spratt, an
electrician from Cincinnati. He noticed dogs eating
leftover hardtack, the dry biscuits sailors ate on long
trips, and figured dog owners could use a product
with a long shelf life for their pets. He created "Meat
Fibrine Dog Cakes," the first dog food of its kind.

Kiss

(ˈkis)

When a dog licks another dog or a human as a show of affection. Licking a human or another dog's face is an instinctual social behavior. Dog kisses are used in a pack as a way of showing you are part of the dog's family. If your dog kisses your face when you come home, it's telling you it's glad to see you—or it may just like the salty taste of your skin.

Who Knew?

Licking/kissing is also a sign of social deference or submission and signals that the dog is not a threat.

Leash Training
('lēsh 'trā-niŋ)

The process of teaching a dog how to walk calmly on a leash. Walking while being tethered doesn't come naturally to most dogs, especially puppies, and the dog is likely to pull, zigzag, jump up or even wrap the leash around your legs. In addition to being super annoying (as anyone who has tried to walk a puppy for more than a block can attest), a dog that pulls and strains can potentially injure themselves or the person holding the other end of the leash.

Who Knew?

Most states or urban districts have local laws that require your dog to be on a leash that is no more than 6 feet long.

Lick
('lik)

To draw the tongue over something. New mothers will lick their puppies to clean them, and adult dogs will groom themselves with their tongues or lick as a way to feel calm or self-soothe. But a dog may also lick its skin if it's itchy, if there's a wound or sore spot, or if it is feeling pain. Puppies lick out of instinct to gather information about the world around them.

Who Knew?

While there's some evidence that a dog's saliva may have some antibacterial and antimicrobial properties, excessively licking an area can cause a "hot spot" and/or an infection to develop. (Enter the dreaded "dog cone," which can prevent a dog from interfering with a wound while it heals.)

Microchip

('mī-krō-ˌchip)

A radio-frequency identification (RFID) device the size of a grain of rice that can be implanted into a dog (or cat) just under the skin between the shoulder blades and neck. It provides permanent identification so if the animal becomes lost, it can be identified and returned to its owner. Each chip has a unique number, which is detected using a scanner. Microchip companies maintain an owner's contact information in their databases, so it's important to keep this information updated.

Who Knew?

A study published in the *Journal of the American Veterinary Medical Association* of more than 7,700 stray animals at shelters showed that dogs without microchips were returned to their owners 21.9% of the time, whereas microchipped dogs were returned to their owners 52.2% of the time.

Mixed Breed
('mikst 'brēd)

A domesticated dog descended from multiple breeds (also called "mutt"). Because they have a more diverse genetic pool with less inbreeding, mixed breeds are often healthier than purebred dogs, that may have more genetic health issues, breed-specific temperaments and behavior compulsions such as herding or hunting. With mixed-breed dogs (that make up more than 50% of the U.S. dog population and are widely available at shelters and through rescue groups), it's really anyone's guess what personality type might dominate!

Who Knew?

The dog community differentiates between "crossbreeds," which are a mix of two purebred dogs (otherwise known as "designer dogs" such as labradoodles or cockapoos) and mixed breeds, which are a cross of three or more breeds.

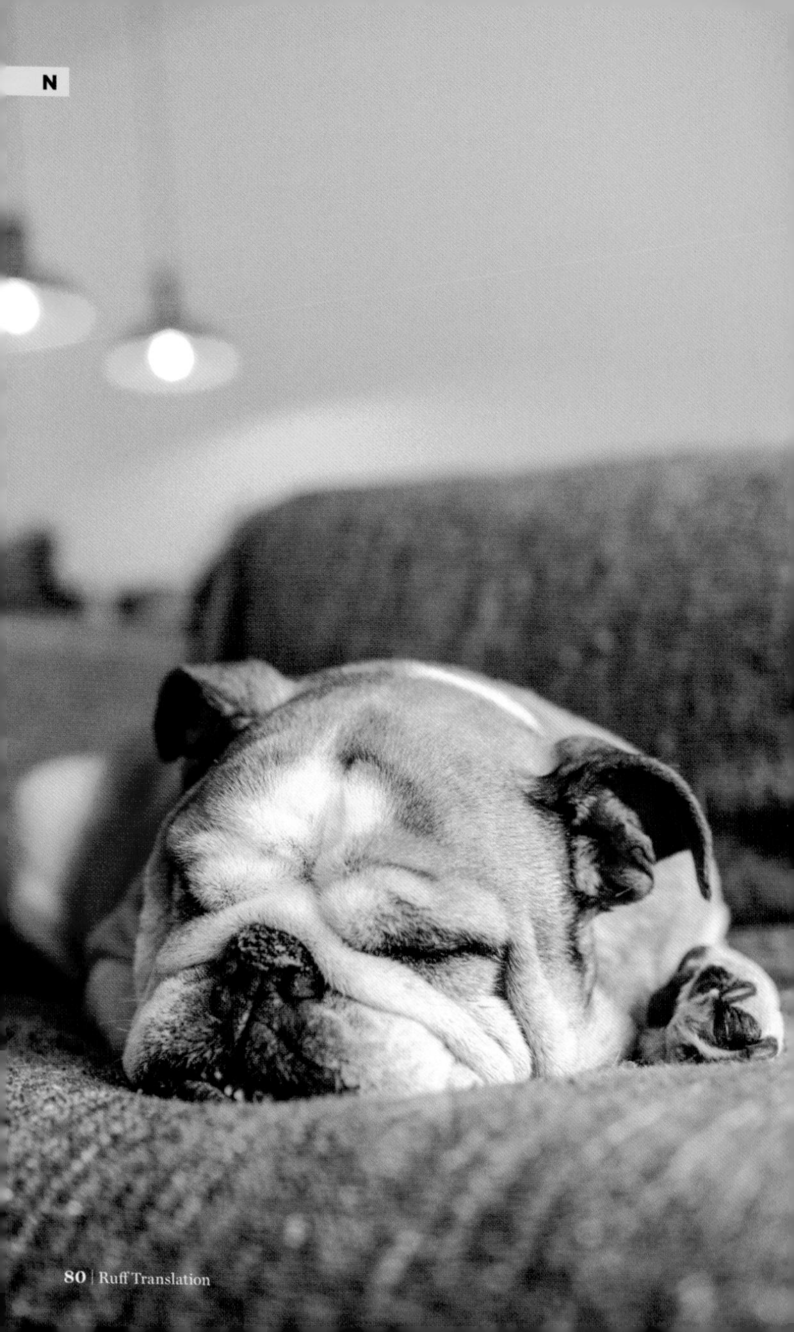

Nap

('nap)

To sleep briefly (or not so briefly) during the day. Since dogs don't need to use alarm clocks to get up early for work or appointments, they are able to sleep whenever their bodies need it. But even active, energetic dogs need to nap often. Large breeds use more energy just to keep moving, so they sleep to recuperate. Puppies and young dogs are active in bursts of manic energy, usually followed by a snooze. Older dogs nap frequently to help their bodies heal and recover from daily activity.

Who Knew?

Studies show that dogs sleep on average about 50% of the time, or about 12 hours a day.

Nature vs. Nurture

('nā-chər 'vər-səs 'nər-chər)

A debate whether behavior and temperament are determined by the environment (either prenatal or during a dog's life), or by the animal's genes. Genetics generally affect temperament, or what the dog is born with, while life experiences affect personality and behavior. Even elements such as the amount of the mother's stress hormones can result in puppies that are more reactive to stress (nature), while puppies separated from their mother too early may be prone to separation anxiety (nurture).

Who Knew?

Darwin's Ark, a research consortium, classifies five inherent traits that affect a dog's personality: food motivation, energy level, confidence level, play drive and sociability.

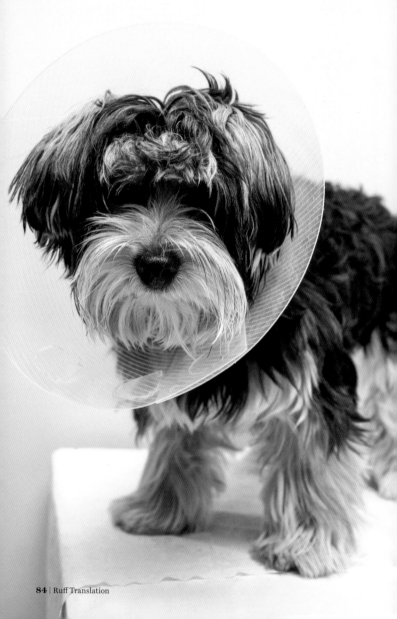

Neuter

('nü-tər)

A surgical procedure that removes the testes from a male dog. Dogs that are neutered cannot reproduce. Performed under general anesthesia, the operation usually takes no more than 15 or 20 minutes, and most vets use absorbable internal sutures, so dogs don't need a repeat visit to have them removed. Neutering a dog helps prevent testicular cancer and reduces the risk of prostate disease, as well as curbs behavioral issues including aggressive behavior.

Who Knew?

Healthy dogs can be neutered when they're as young as 6 months of age.

Nose

('nōz)

The front part of the head that's involved in breathing and smelling. In a dog, a portion of air that's inhaled goes directly to a recessed area in the back of the nose that processes odor; the rest flows down to the lungs. The membrane that absorbs odors spreads across a maze of bone structures and routes the molecules based on their chemical properties. This allows dogs to process different smells. With 300 million scent receptors, a dog has a sense of smell estimated to be between 100,000 and 100 million times more sensitive than a human's.

Who Knew?

A dog's nose print is as unique as a human fingerprint and can be used for identification. The Canadian Kennel Club has been accepting nose prints as proof of identity since 1938!

Nutrition

(nŭ-ˈtri-shən)

The act or process of being nourished. Dogs require a mix of six major nutrients: protein, fat, carbohydrates, vitamins, minerals and water. Dogs digest protein more efficiently from animal products than plant proteins. They also need fatty acids, carbs from vegetables and fruit (or very well-cooked grains), and a balance of vitamins and minerals. Read labels and avoid commercial dog food that contains byproducts, artificial preservatives and added sweeteners. Meat should be in two of the top three ingredients in commercial dog food.

Who Knew?

Look for the AAFCO (Association of American Feed Control Officials) seal on the food you buy your pup; the organization sets minimum nutritional pet food standards that companies must meet.

Obedience Training

(ō-'bē-dē-ən(t)s 'trā-niŋ)

Training a puppy or dog in the basic commands and appropriate behavior. Using positive reinforcement, dogs can learn to sit, stay, lie down and come on command, as well as what not to do (jump up, sniff someone's crotch, bark incessantly at the pizza delivery person...). A few common steps to follow: Keep your practice sessions frequent and short (no longer than 15 minutes at a time). Use rewards that your dog really likes (chicken; freeze-dried liver bits). And never, ever use punishment, including yelling or hitting. It'll just upset a dog and make it scared of you.

Who Knew?

Be patient: You can't expect a dog to know something it hasn't yet learned—just like you wouldn't expect a toddler to know how to tie a shoe.

Obesity

(ō-'bē-sə-tē)

A condition characterized by excessive body fat that increases the risk of health problems, including arthritis and joint issues; bladder, urinary tract, kidney and liver disease; diabetes; heart failure; and high blood pressure. As with humans, the best approach to weight loss for a dog is one that targets fat loss while preserving lean muscle mass. (Meaning, more exercise and less food and treats.) Follow food label guidelines for determining the correct amount for your pooch, and adjust accordingly based on its activity level.

Who Knew?

Nearly 37% of dogs in the U.S. are classified as overweight and about 19% are considered to be obese, according to the Association for Pet Obesity Prevention.

Oxytocin

(äk-si-ˈtō-sᵊn)

A neurotransmitter known as the "love hormone," it enters the bloodstream and causes feelings of bonding and connection; it also positively affects social cognition and behavior. Studies have shown that oxytocin may be involved in the bonding between dogs and humans following positive social interactions. Oxytocin is common to the formation of both romantic and parental social bonds, providing scientific evidence that we love our dogs just like we love people.

Who Knew?

A 2015 study in the journal *Science* found that after humans and dogs looked into each other's eyes during a 30-minute period, oxytocin increased in both parties.

Pant
('pant)

To breathe hard and quickly with the mouth open and tongue out. Dogs have very few sweat glands, so they pant as a way to release heat and cool down. But that's not the only reason for that rapid breathing: Dogs can also pant because they are feeling stressed, afraid or anxious—or, paradoxically, happy or playful. Reading your dog's body language can help you figure out why it's panting. A few health problems may also make a dog pant, including pain, a high temperature, a respiratory disorder or heart failure.

Who Knew?

When dogs inhale rapidly, they use the evaporation of moisture from their mouths and tongue to exchange hot air from their lungs for cooler external air, lowering their temperature from the inside out.

Paw

('pȯ)

The foot of a dog or other animal. The pads of the paws are made of fatty tissue that protect the feet from both cold and hot surfaces as well as rough terrain. A system of arteries and veins run through a dog's paw pads, helping to maintain a constant temperature, even when exposed to extremely cold conditions. However, paws can get frostbite from long exposure or burns from walking on very hot surfaces such as sidewalks or sand.

Who Knew?

One of the few places that dogs have sweat glands is in their paws. When a dog is stressed—like when going to the vet—you may see a trail of wet paw prints.

Personality

(ˌpər-sə-ˈna-lə-tē)

The essential character. To some extent breed influences personality, but every individual dog has its own unique characteristics. Genetically, certain breed groups (such as terriers, toy dogs and working dogs) tend to share similar personality traits, while mixed-breed dogs have personalities that are more individually based. A dog's personality isn't fixed at birth, though—research shows it can change over time, and just like with humans, when dogs go through big changes in life or traumatic experiences, it affects their disposition.

Who Knew?

Dogs and humans may share similar personality traits, according to a study in *Applied Animal Behaviour Science*, which concluded that people have a tendency to select animals that complement their own personalities.

Pet

('pet)

To stroke in a gentle, loving manner. Many dogs like to be petted in particular areas by people they know, but not necessarily by strangers. Petting should always be gentle, rather than vigorous, with the goal of relaxing the dog. You'll know your dog appreciates it when it keeps ducking its head under your hand or pawing you for more love and attention. Top spots include the neck, the base of the tail and the back—just don't thump the head!

Who Knew?

Research shows that when subjects greeted their dogs using both voice and touch, the dogs had much higher levels of the feel-good hormone oxytocin, compared to when they were greeted with just the voice.

Pitch

('pich)

The highness or lowness of a sound. The pitch of a dog's vocalizations may indicate whether it is happy, sad, frightened, threatened, angry or upset. But pitch isn't everything: Low-pitched growls may typically indicate anger or imminent aggression, for example, but low-pitched moans can indicate pleasure and contentment. A high-pitched whine may indicate that a dog means no harm and is safe to approach, especially if it's paired with a wagging tail.

Who Knew?

Humans can also use pitch to communicate with our canine friends. For example, use a high-pitched sound to indicate you don't mean harm if you're approaching a new dog.

Play Bow
('plā 'baů)

The body posture that dogs use to indicate to other canines and humans that they want to play. The typical pose has the dog's front paws stretched out and upper body low, leaning on its elbows, with its rear end elevated. The posture is a way of inviting another dog to play or to simply communicate that they are being friendly. Sometimes, dogs will stop midromp to play bow, reassuring their companion and inviting them to continue gallivanting about.

Who Knew?

Play bows are done to assure the other dog that any rough play is not meant to be aggressive.

Puppy
('pə-pē)

A dog is considered a puppy up to the age of 1 year. However, puppylike behavior may continue until 2 years of age or older, at which point it reaches emotional maturity and develops its adult temperament. Most young dogs have a ton of excess energy and tend to get into everything, so just as you would with a toddler or young child, be sure to puppy-proof your home and don't let a puppy roam your home unattended.

Who Knew?

Puppies should ideally stay with their mom and littermates for eight to 10 weeks, but it's also important during that time for humans to begin the socialization process.

Quick
('kwik)

The core of the nail that contains nerves and blood vessels. A dog with light-colored nails has a pink quick in the center of the nail bed. In dark or black nails, the quick is a bit harder to spot: Turn the paw so you're gazing at the underside of the nail and look for the groove where the hard nail turns to a softer inner tissue. If you see a black dot in the middle of the end, that's the quick. When trimming a dog's nails, trim black nails a little at time, looking at the cut end after snipping so you don't accidentally cut the quick—it can be very painful for your pet.

Who Knew?

If you cut into the quick, the nail will bleed—sometimes a lot. Try dipping the nail into styptic powder to stop the bleeding, or apply a moist cotton applicator with moderate pressure for around 30 seconds. Reapply powder if it's still bleeding.

Rabies

('rā-bēz)

A fatal but preventable viral disease that is usually transmitted through the bite or scratch of a rabid animal. Rabies attacks the nervous system, causing brain inflammation and damaging the muscle tissue, spinal cord and brain. In dogs, the incubation period (the time before symptoms first appear) is two weeks to four months. Dogs that have been vaccinated for rabies and are exposed to the disease will need an additional booster dose, and will need to be quarantined. Dogs that have not been vaccinated and are suspected of being infected with rabies are usually euthanized or die within five days of the onset of symptoms.

Who Knew?

There is no cure for rabies, and it is almost always fatal, which is why vaccination is required by law in most states.

Separation Anxiety

(ˌse-pə-ˈrā-shən aŋ-ˈzī-ə-tē)

A condition in which dogs exhibit extreme stress when left alone. Behavioral veterinarian Andrea Tu describes it as an unreasonable panic. Symptoms include panting, trembling, howling, destructive behavior, accidents in the house, drooling and desperate attempts to escape confinement, which can result in serious injury. A behaviorist can help provide strategies to help your dog feel more secure when you are not home, and some anti-anxiety medications may be useful until the dog learns to relax.

Who Knew?

Never punish a dog for making a mess when left alone, as this will only make the anxiety worse.

Shed

('shed)

To lose dead or damaged hair so healthy new fur can grow. Some breeds shed year-round, others shed seasonally in spring and fall, and some shed very little or not at all. It's important to brush dogs that shed several times a week—or daily, during heavy shedding periods. Stress, allergies, poor-quality food and some medical conditions can also cause excessive shedding. Talk to your veterinarian about underlying conditions, nutrition and the best tools to use for grooming.

Who Knew?

The amount of shedding depends largely on breed; dogs with double coats (such as chow chows, Labrador retrievers and German shepherds) tend to shed the most.

s

Sniff

('snif)

To inhale through the nose to smell something. Dogs experience the world through smell, and scent is how dogs communicate on a primitive level, both by leaving their scent and sniffing out other dogs. Allowing dogs to sniff on their walks provides mental stimulation, boosts their mood and enriches their lives. Just make sure you watch what your pooch is sniffing so it doesn't get near anything toxic (or completely disgusting).

Who Knew?

When a dog's nose is wet and cold, it can more easily detect odors, due to glands that produce an oily fluid.

Socialization

(ˌsō-sh(ə-)lə-ˈzā-shən)

The process of introducing a puppy or dog to different people, animals, places, sights, sounds and experiences in a positive way. Socialization prepares a young dog to be part of society and coexist happily with humans and other animals. Socialization shapes a dog's future personality and the way it reacts to its environment as an adult. The process of socialization helps a dog become well-adjusted and prevents unreasonable fears, such as a fear of children or riding in a car.

Who Knew?

Puppies are most open to socialization from 3 weeks to 16 weeks of age, but you can still help a dog socialize at any age.

Spay

('spā)

A surgical procedure that removes the ovaries and uterus from a female dog (although some vets are now removing only the ovaries). Spaying makes a dog unable to reproduce and eliminates its heat cycle and mating-related behavior. Most veterinarians recommend spaying a dog between 4 months and 6 months of age. The surgery is performed under general anesthesia, and the incision is closed by stitches under the skin that are eventually absorbed by the body.

Who Knew?

Spaying reduces the risk of breast cancer and uterine infections, particularly if the procedure is done before a dog's first heat.

Tail

('tāl)

A flexible appendage at the rear of a dog. The tail is an extension of a dog's backbone and consists of between six and 23 vertebrae (depending on the breed), which are enclosed in muscles that help it move up, down and from side to side. The tail plays some role in movement and balance, but its most important function is in communication, whether it's a signal of how happy your dog is to see you (tail upright), or how stressed it is feeling at the sight of another dog (tail between the legs).

Who Knew?

Tails can also play a number of other roles, depending on the breed. Nordic and Arctic dogs pull their bushy tails across their faces to keep out the cold when lying down. Water dogs use their strong, thick tails as rudders while swimming. And speedy dogs such as sighthounds (greyhounds; whippets) use their tails to help change direction at high velocity.

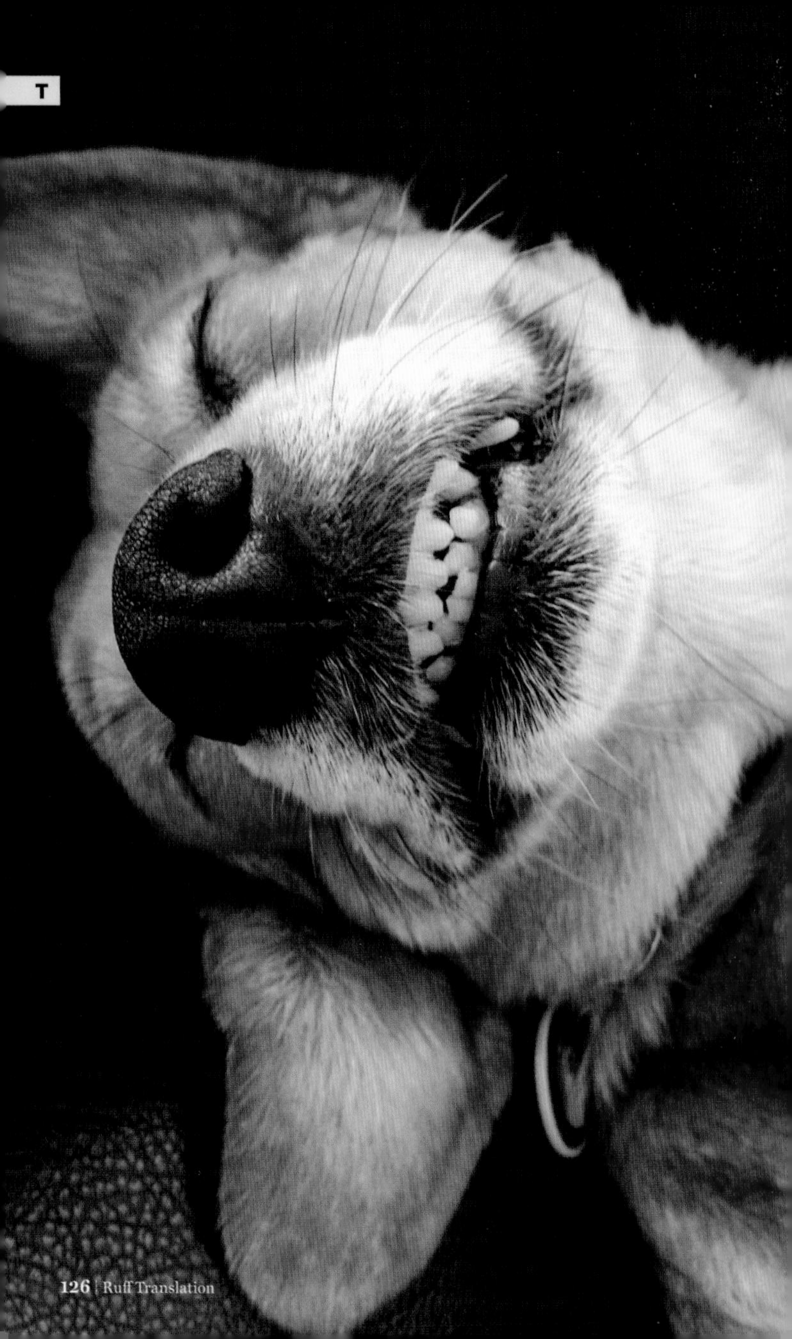

Teeth
('tēth)

The hard projections attached to the jaws. A puppy has 28 teeth (also called milk teeth), which come in at around 2 weeks of age and are completely grown in at 8 to 10 weeks. The incisors usually fall out at about 4 months, followed by the canine teeth, when the dog is between 5 to 6 months old. They are replaced by 42 adult teeth. Caring for your dog's teeth is important for their overall well-being, as well as preventing the pain of dental disease. Brushing and annual dental cleaning at the vet will help maintain a dog's pearly whites and oral health.

Who Knew?

A dog's adult teeth include incisors, for biting; canines, for tearing and shredding; and molars, for shearing and crushing.

Tongue

('tən)

The movable, muscular organ in the mouth.
A dog uses its tongue to drink water, lap
up food, clean its body, kiss its humans
and regulate its temperature. When a dog
exercises, its tongue enlarges with increased
blood flow, and it may hang out of the dog's
mouth. The air exposure causes the moisture
on the tongue to evaporate and cools blood
flow, helping release excess heat. Dogs
only have about a sixth of the taste buds as
humans, but they can still taste things that
are sour, bitter, salty and sweet.

Who Knew?

A dog's tongue influences the way it barks;
the size and shape of its tongue helps create
its unique pitch and tone.

Toys

('tȯiz)

Objects to play with. Toys are important to a dog's well-being, providing mental stimulation, comfort and exercise. They're also a good way to stave off boredom and prevent destructive behavior when your pooch is home alone. You'll find playthings designed for different needs, from balls for exercise, to soft stuffed animals for comfort, to puzzle games for mental stimulation. Just remember to use size-appropriate options to prevent choking and supervise your dog when toys have parts that can be removed and swallowed (like squeakers).

Who Knew?

Consider color and environment when choosing a dog's toy. Since canines have vision similar to that of a human with red-green color blindness, a dog may not be able to find a red ball in green grass.

Treats

('trētz)

Small pieces of tasty food given primarily as a reward (as in training your dog to sit and stay) or reinforcing a positive behavior (like not jumping up on a visitor). For training purposes, stick to small amounts of high-reward foods; if you're trying to keep your dog distracted or engaged, look for chewy treats such as bully sticks. Consider your dog's size and chew strength when picking out treats for your pup.

Who Knew?

To prevent weight gain, treats should make up no more than 10% of your dog's daily caloric needs.

Unconditional Love

(ˌən-kən-ˈdish-nəl ˈləv)

A bond that exists without any limits or qualifications. Dogs love their humans unconditionally. A study by scientists at Emory University found that dogs and humans have the same "reward center" in the brain associated with positive emotions, and dogs respond differently when given a treat by someone they love rather than a stranger. Humans who are able to love their dogs unconditionally—despite a dog's bad behavior, illness or old age—will reap the biggest benefits from this bond.

Who Knew?

Therapy dogs are some of the best examples of animals that give love and affection unconditionally. They can be trained to work with special populations, such as children with autism or patients in hospitals, as a way to provide comfort and care.

Vaccine
(vak-'sēn)

A biological preparation that provides active acquired immunity to an infectious disease. Many fatal diseases—including rabies, distemper and parvo—are now preventable because of vaccines. The rabies vaccine is legally required in most states. Other core vaccines recommended for all dogs by the American Animal Hospital Association include those for distemper virus, canine parvovirus and canine adenovirus-2 (hepatitis); vaccines for leptospirosis, Lyme disease, parainfluenza, kennel cough and canine influenza are also recommended.

Who Knew?

Puppies should get a series of vaccinations over three vet visits starting when the dog is between 6 and 8 weeks old.

Veterinarian

(ˌve-tə-rə-ˈner-ē-ən)

A person who has been trained in the science of animal medicine. Regular preventive veterinary care along with nutritious food, exercise and companionship will help keep dogs healthy. Adult dogs should see the vet at least once a year for a complete checkup, while puppies will need to go every three or four weeks up to 4 months old, and seniors (over age 8) should get a checkup twice a year. Choose a veterinarian that you feel comfortable asking for advice, who reliably returns your phone calls and whose "bedside manner" makes your dog comfortable.

Who Knew?

Veterinarians generally devote eight years to their education, including four years in college and four years in graduate school earning a degree as a doctor of veterinary medicine (DVM).

Walk

('wȯk)

A daily walking excursion in which dogs exercise, eliminate and explore. Dogs need to go outside and walk every day. Going for a stroll provides an outlet for your pooch to burn off excess energy, helps it maintain a healthy weight and gives it a chance for a little nose-to-ground exploration. Plus, dogs are social animals, and many welcome the opportunity to meet and greet other dogs as part of their day. You don't need to spend hours holding the leash—aim for about 30 minutes a day of walking.

Who Knew?

Humans benefit from daily walks with their dogs, too! Dog owners are about four times more likely than other people to meet today's physical activity guidelines of at least 150 minutes of moderate physical activity a week, according to a recent British study.

Whine

('(h)wīn)

A prolonged, high-pitched noise. Among other sounds, dogs use whining to communicate with their humans. The sound is often used to get attention, but sometimes it indicates anxiety, stress, pain, fear—or just a signal that your pup wants something (like a ball that's stuck under the couch). Body language can provide some context: A dog that is whining while wagging its tail, licking a person or following another dog or human around may just want some attention. A dog whimpering by the front door probably needs to go out.

Who Knew?

Dogs will often whine when they are in pain, so if you start to notice your animal whimpering or crying out frequently, consult your vet to make sure there's not a medical issue going on.

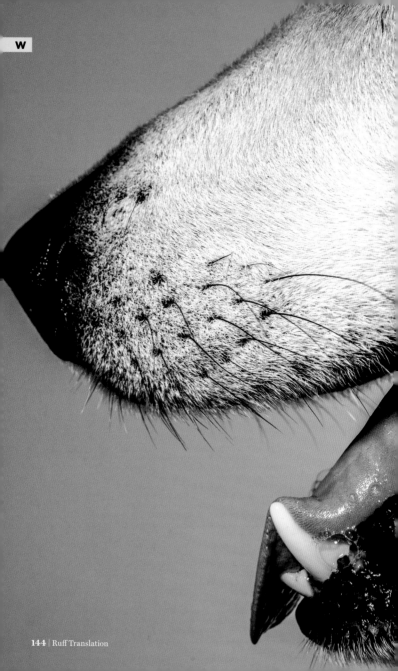

Whiskers

('(h)wi-skərz)

The long, projecting stiff hairs growing on the sides of a dog's muzzle. Whiskers help a dog navigate its environment by providing additional sensory input. They detect the size, shape, speed and movement of objects, as well as subtle changes in air currents that bounce off solid objects. Whiskers can help dogs find things in the dark. In the wild, they can alert a dog to prey or potential enemies. They even help dogs determine whether they can fit through narrow spaces.

Who Knew?

Dogs are naturally farsighted, so whiskers help give them additional information about things that are up close.

Wolves

('wŭlvz)

Large carnivorous canids of the genus *Canis*. All dogs (*Canis familiaris*) are descendants of a now-extinct subspecies of the gray wolf (*Canis lupus*), although scientists differ on just how long ago and where in the world this evolution took place. In 2017, research from Stony Brook University narrowed the first domestication of dogs to 20,000–40,000 years ago. Scientists speculate that this domestication first took place in Asia and that some time after, the lineages split into East Asian and Western Eurasian dogs.

Who Knew?

While they share many of the same genes as dogs, wolves typically have a larger head, narrower chest and hips, longer legs and bigger paws—all of which help them cover more ground (up to 50 miles a day). They also have yellow or amber eyes, versus a dog's blue, green or brown peepers.

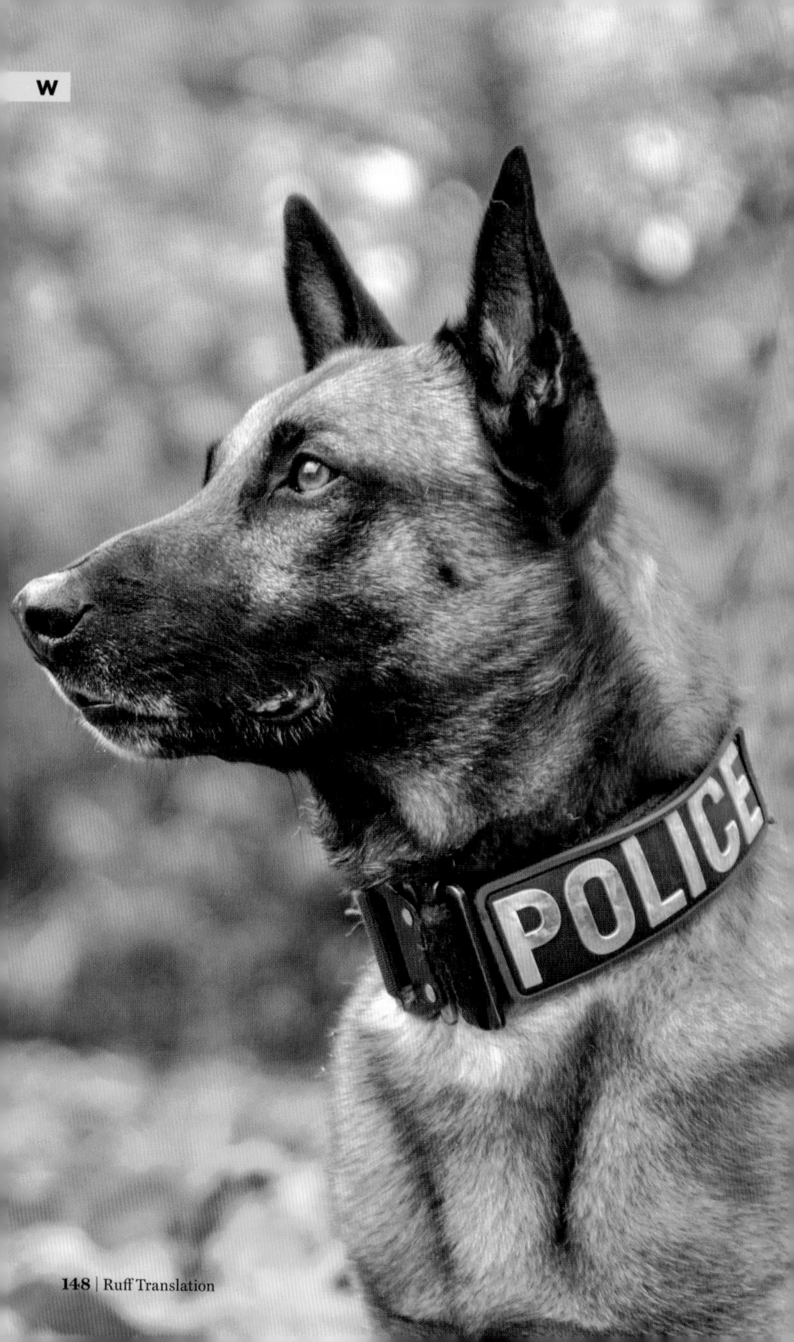
POLICE

Working Dogs

(ˈwər-kiŋ ˈdägz)

Dogs that are bred to perform tasks and assist humans. Some dog breeds have been bred over the centuries to do dedicated work, such as herding sheep or cattle. But the definition of working dog has expanded greatly beyond specific breeds to include animals that are trained for certain jobs, whether that's working as a guide dog, taking part in search-and-rescue efforts, helping law enforcement with tasks such as drug or explosives detection, or medical-alert dogs that can help signal seizures and other health concerns in their humans.

Who Knew?

The American Kennel Club recognizes 31 breeds in the Working Group, including popular ones such as the boxer, Doberman pinscher and Siberian husky.

Xtreme Dog Sports

(ik-'strēm 'däg 'spȯrtz)

A group of high-impact sports that dogs play and compete in. Events include dock-diving (competing for the longest jump); agility (navigating a course including jumps, tunnels, teeter boards and other obstacles); flyball (two teams of dogs race over hurdles toward a "flyball box," which releases a tennis ball that has to be brought back to the finish line); lure-coursing (chasing a lure on a wire to compete for the fastest speed); disc dog (catching a flying disc and choreographed freestyle catching); and more.

Who Knew?

The American Kennel Club recently passed regulations allowing mixed-breed dogs to take part in agility, tracking and obedience competitions—events that were once limited only to purebred dogs.

Yawn

('yȯn)

The process of opening the mouth wide and taking a deep breath. Yawning is usually an involuntary reaction to fatigue or boredom in humans and dogs alike, but in canines it can also indicate discomfort, especially if your dog is licking its lips. Dogs also yawn to deflect a threat and avoid conflict when confronted by an aggressive animal. Just watch out—if your animal is yawning repeatedly in rapid succession, it may be feeling anxious, stressed or overwhelmed.

Who Knew?

A recent study found that human yawning is contagious to dogs, which seem to yawn out of empathy.

Zooeyia

(zoo-'ī -uh)

The positive benefits to human health from interacting with animals. These benefits include a reduced risk of cardiovascular disease; lower blood pressure and cholesterol levels; decreased stress, loneliness and depression; and even better surgical recovery rates. Getting out of your house to walk your dog or head to the park provides more physical activity and can also help prevent feelings of isolation, improve your social life and increase human-to-human interaction.

Who Knew?

Researchers at the worldwide One Health Initiative coined the term zooeyia from the Greek root words for animal (zoion) and health (from the Greek goddess of health, Hygeia).

INDEX

CREDITS

SPECIAL THANKS TO CONTRIBUTING WRITER

Pamela Weintraub

CENTENNIAL BOOKS

An Imprint of
Centennial Media, LLC
40 Worth St., 10th Floor
New York, NY 10013, U.S.A.

ISBN 978-1-951274-73-3

Distributed by
Simon & Schuster, Inc.
1230 Avenue of the Americas
New York, NY 10020, U.S.A.

For information about custom editions, special sales and
premium and corporate purchases, please contact Centennial Media
at contact@centennialmedia.com.

Manufactured in China